Johanna Elisabet
An Angel is Born
A Story of Love, Loss and Hope

Johanna Elisabeth Sather, R.N.

An Angel is Born

A Story of Love, Loss and Hope

Bluestar Communications®
Woodside, CA

Copyright © 2000 Johanna Elisabeth Sather
Published by:
Bluestar Communications
44 Bear Glenn
Woodside, CA. 94062
Tel: 800-6-BLUESTAR (800-625-8378)

Illustrations: © 2000 Johanna Elisabeth Sather

Edited by Caryn Summers
Layout by Petra Michel
First Printing 2000
ISBN: 1-885394-39-X

Library of Congress Cataloging-in-Publication Data

Sather, Johanna Elisabeth, 1940-
   An angel is born : a story of love, loss, and hope / Johanna Elisabeth Sather.
      p. cm.
   Includes bibliographical references (p.).
   ISBN 1-885394-39-X
   I. Title.
PS3569.A7694A84   1999
813'.54--dc21   99-35300
                                                                                       CIP

All rights reserved. No part of this book may be reproduced in any form without the written permission of the publishers, except for brief quotations embodied in critical articles and reviews.

Printed in USA

Contents

Acknowledgments 7
An Angel is Born 8
Appendix 61
Resource List 63
    Support Groups 63
    Associations and Newsletters 65
Recommended Reading 67
Quote References 69

Dedicated to Brennan Dane Stow
September 5, 1995 - April 5, 1996

Acknowledgments

I watched a baby die in his father's arms. The experience pierced me, leaving behind a kernel that, watered by my imagination and the therapy of writing, flourished and grew into this work.

When they heard of my effort, the baby's parents asked, please, could they read it. With great hesitancy, I sent a copy to them, knowing I had taken liberties to embellish their story with my own renderings and fanciful ideas. And after all, I had known their child but one day; they had endured months of angst watching their baby fail.

My thanks to those parents, Lynda and Dane Stow, for loving the story, for their inspiration and support, for the kindnesses they have shown me along the way. I admire them for the graceful way they are traveling through this passage, and are guiding their remaining son through the loss of his brother.

I am grateful for Ann Williams, R.N., who worked beside me that evening and shared a poignant experience with me.

Thanks to Jackie Silva for the many proof readings, valued comments and advice–few people will critique a friend's work, over and over again.

Caryn Summers, my editor and friend, thank you for your skill and wisdom in editing. You have added clarity and enhanced the flow of the words while leaving my story intact. You believed in this work and gave it wings.

And finally my profound gratitude to Petra Michel, my publisher, for bringing this book to fruition. The cover design and charming page layout bears witness to your creative gift. Many thanks to you, Petra.

Life is short and we never have enough time for gladdening the hearts of those who are traveling the dark journey with us. O, be swift to love, make haste to be kind.

Henri Frédéric Amiel

Brennan's ending was written even before he was pulled from his mother's thighs, his return passage purchased at conception. An

error chanced in his cells, deep within the spiraling helices of genetic information that spelled out characteristics unique to him… the soft of his hair, the cream of his skin, the blue of his eyes, the sweet rosebud of a mouth that could on occasion push to an indignant pout. The error spawned the rigid labor of his seizures, the suspension of his development, the brevity of his stay.

In the last hours of his life, the lean season of our acquaintance, Brennan reached into my heart and opened a door I did not know was there… I, who am rarely drawn to babies and small children, I, who was wheeled into the delivery room long ago silently lamenting, "What am I to do with a baby?"… only to be saved by nature's protective hormones that transform unready young women into fierce protective mothers.

All I have seen teaches me to trust the Creator for all I have not seen.

Ralph Waldo Emerson

And I, who had never before longed for grandchildren, had recently begun yearning for a baby, asking for a baby in my life again. I did not expect it to come in the way it did.

The day is Good Friday. "You should take the patient in 254," I am advised when I arrive for the afternoon shift at the hospital where I work as a nurse.

"Why, what's the problem?"

"It's complicated," the day

nurse replies, obviously strained at the end of her watch. I do not press her for she has already turned to move away, but I take her cue and assign myself to that room.

As the off-going shift reports to the oncoming, the story unfolds. The patient in room 254 is a young man who had his gallbladder removed three days earlier. The surgeons had employed a condensed procedure wherein a laparoscope is inserted through a minute incision; the gall bladder is seized, severed and withdrawn through the same incision. Very slick, go for the target and minimize disruption of adjacent terrain— makes for a speedy recovery. But at home in the aftermath of his surgery, the young man was seized by spasms of urgent pain, not to be assuaged by the pills he obediently swallowed.

The man returned to the clinic for evaluation and was admitted to the hospital for intravenous therapy: IV fluids

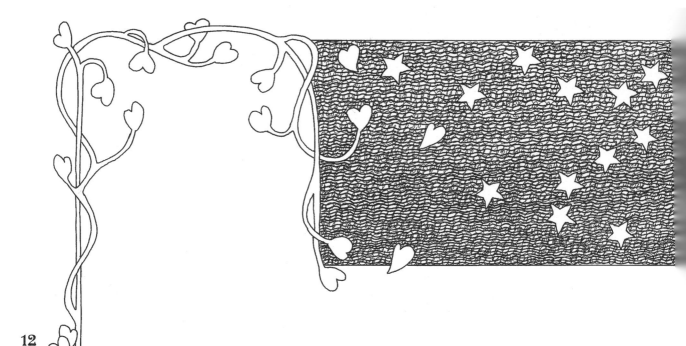

In grief we know the worst of what we feel, But who can tell the end of what we fear?

Hannah More

to rest his belly, bold analgesics to quell the insistent pain, antibiotics for good measure.

A thorough *history and physical* has been dictated, typed and filed in his chart. It lists a battery of statistics that indicate his height and weight, his vital signs, pertinent past diseases and other medical history. His alcohol and tobacco usage are ascertained, his life style and oc-

cupation are accounted for as well as his marital status. His blood chemistries and other serum counts are itemized along with the results of diagnostic procedures. His current condition is detailed and summarized, and a plan for treatment is recommended. But nowhere in the two page, single spaced, typewritten document is a hint that this patient's seven-month-old son is dying, whose death, in fact, is imminent. There is not a breath of it. Western medicine has a curious case of tunnel vision.

Brennan was a September baby, now approaching the end of his seventh month. Second born child to a couple who, after many years, had resigned themselves to barrenness. But as it sometimes happens with adoption plans underway, they

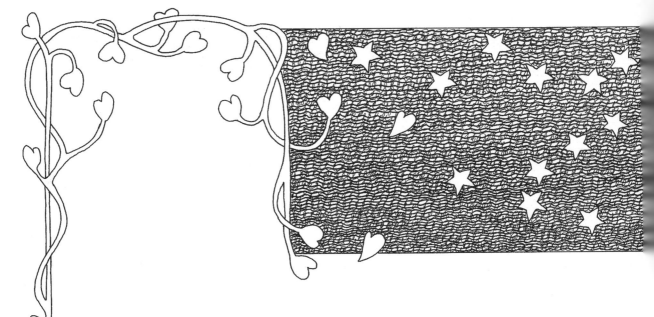

*Calm me, my God,
 and keep me calm,
While these hot
 breezes blow:
Be like the nightdew's
 cooling balm
Upon earth's fevered
 brow.*

Horatius Bonar

were surprised with a pregnancy that produced a son, and three years later, another.

Brennan was a normal healthy newborn… well, he seemed so. Oh, there were those little nags one pushes to the rear of the line, but as six weeks drew to a close, the nags took on an ominous tone, and his parents were duly advised their infant son would not survive. His body was never in-

tended to blossom into a child's, mature to manhood. Brennan's would be an abbreviated life, a promise unfulfilled.

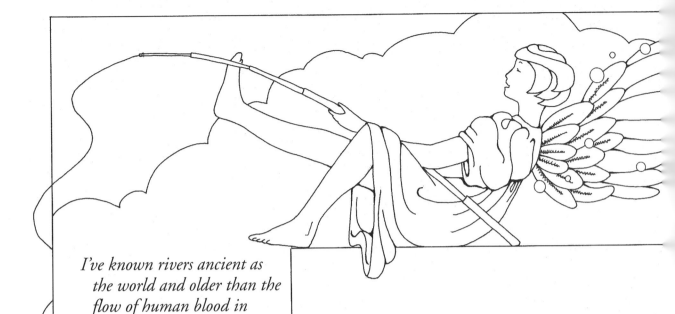

I've known rivers ancient as the world and older than the flow of human blood in human veins.

My soul has grown deep like the rivers.

*I bathed in the Euphrates when dawns were young.
I built my hut near the Congo and it lulled me to sleep.
I looked upon the Nile and raised the pyramids above it.
I heard the singing of the Mississippi when Abe Lincoln went down to New Orleans, and I've seen its muddy bosom turn all golden in the sunset.*

I've known rivers: Ancient, dusky rivers.

My soul has grown deep like the rivers.

Langston Hughes

Brennan loved life, whether he experienced it as an angel in the realms of spirit, or with a human heart

in the heavy fabric of physicality. He had lived many lives on Earth, indeed too many to count. He had come as tribesmen to the plains of Africa, as traveling merchants in the ancient east, as silent monks and as beautiful women, as lusty barbarians, as slaves, as slave keepers, as lepers, as kings, as beggars, as women of the night. The lives were intense or mundane, woeful and brief, or full of years, steeped in joy and adventure depending upon the birth setting and the choices made thereafter. He had run the gamut and exhausted the characters. In fact, he had suffered and savored so many lives that he had fulfilled his mission in the galaxy wherein Earth roams. He had felt every anguish and pain and fury until, at last, he remembered the love from which his soul was spun.

The divine spark is within us all and when we are conscious of it, we touch the eternal…

Sigurd Olson

The blue of heaven is larger than the clouds.

Elizabeth Barrett Browning

Now he comes only on cameo appearances to lend assistance to those he has loved in other times, in other realms, in other roles. And now when he comes to Earth, he does not fully lose the memory of his angelhood.

Wasn't it only yesterday in the realm of angels when he and his noble friends gathered together in the Celestial Chamber of Planning… the very friends who sit now in

the hospital room as the mother and father and brother of the baby Brennan?

Brennan's eternal name is difficult to say within the limitations of matter, for its consonants are far more exquisite than human tongues can mimic, its vowels greater than mere connecting sounds; they are heard as music, felt as emotion and seen as a dancing spectrum of light. Each name sets its own mood, sings its song in its own distinctive color. But for now we will call him Brennan for the sake of convenience and pretend we see the lights.

On that day in the realm of angels, Brennan and his friends assembled with the Great Casting Counsel for the purpose of planning new experiences for learning in the physical. There was much laughter and merriment, for angels remember

It is said—and it is true—that just before we are born, a cavern angel holds his finger to our mouths and whispers, "Hush! Don't tell what you know." This is why we have a cleft on our upper lips and remember nothing of where we came from.

Roderick MacLeish

their divine origins and know that life on Earth is temporary, a mere sliver of eternity. They leap into their earthly experiences with great enthusiasm for they know life is too important to take seriously. They will fall prey to seriousness soon enough when they are in the flesh, for matter draws a curtain between the worlds. If humans remembered, they would only wish to return home.

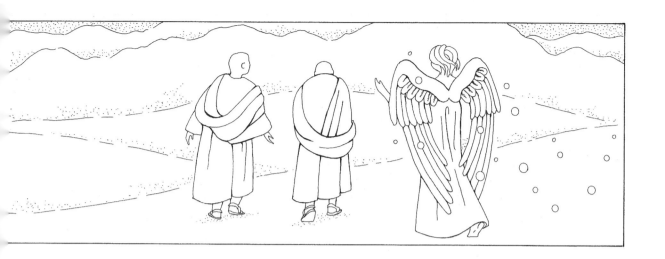

Brennan's friends and the Counsel pondered an assignment which is a most difficult one… the lesson of losing a child, for that is something humans take very seriously. There is a story on Earth of a great master who lived many hundreds of years ago in Tibet. It happened that the master's son died and the great teacher was stricken with grief, overcome with the burden of it. Perplexed, his student said to him, "Master, you say this life is but an illusion. I do not understand then, why you grieve so terribly."

With brimming eyes, sad and deep, the teacher replied, "So it is, life on Earth is an illusion. But the death of a child is the greatest illusion of them all."

Amidst merriment and camaraderie, in their spirit bodies Brennan's friends felt no burden or heaviness. "I'll be the

Listen—perhaps you catch a hint of an ancient state not quite forgotten; dim, perhaps, and yet not altogether unfamiliar, like a song whose name is long forgotten, and the circumstances in which you heard completely unremembered. Not the whole song has stayed with you, but just a little wisp of melody, attached not to a person or a place or anything particular.

But you remember, from just this little part, how lovely was the song, how wonderful the setting where you heard it, and how you loved those who were there and listened with you.

A Course in Miracles

dad," one of them said, and another replied, "Well then, I'll be the mother." Another chimed in and said, "Brennan, your lessons are finished, why don't you come with us? You can be the baby. I'll go first and be your brother."

Brennan smiled and said in mock dismay as if he were asked to leave a picnic, "Do I have to?" But then he laughed in the same vein for

he loved his friends much and he said, "I'll come if I do not have to stay too long."

I'll come just for breakfast. Put on the coffee, warm the sweet rolls. We'll visit while the dew glistens like diamonds on the grass, before the crisp of morning softens to warm, while the world is quiet and we still remember our dreams.

*One day out of darkness
they shall meet,
And read life's meaning
in each other's eyes.*

Susan Mark Spalding

Today on this Good Friday afternoon, the mother has brought her children to the hospital, the young boy and the baby. We have created

a dorm of sorts in her husband's room, arranging a fold-up rollaway bed with a lumpy mattress against the wall, and in a little alcove under the room's only window, we install a crib borrowed from the pediatric unit. This is where Brennan lies sleeping when I enter the room to greet and assess his father, my patient. I pass the baby and pause. In an instant my heart is captured by the child almost as if I recognize him. Moments before, a nurse who is my friend had approached me. "I couldn't do what you're doing," she said, shaking her head slowly. And I remember my words for I believed them to be true. "This won't bother me," I said. "I can separate myself from the situation—I won't take this baby home with me."

My training as a nurse has been to distance myself emotionally from the tragedies that abound in my work. But

Who can doubt that we exist only to love? We live not a moment exempt from its influence.

Blaise Pascal

sometimes there are land mines awaiting an unsuspecting footfall. Today the footfall and land mine meet at the side of a baby's crib. And I gaze at the child, enchanted. "You have an angel here," I say to the father. "He has just come to stay with you for a little while." The father knows. He knows. And he feels the anguish of the illusion. Then we speak of medical things,

of surgery and pain and the reasons the father returns to our hospital.

The mother has gone to take the older child home to his grandmother; this room is too small for his energy. It is dinnertime. While my other patients eat, I sit with Brennan and his father. Until all the news is back from the tests and the crisis is past, the father cannot eat. We speak in hushed tones while sterile water laced with glucose and saline and a little potassium drips into his vein. That will be his dinner for tonight. The baby sleeps in the crib covered with a handmade quilt, a gift from a friend at the time of his birth. It is an infant-sized square; the friend did not know that the infant would never outgrow it. A floppy stuffed rabbit slouches in the corner of the crib against the slats.

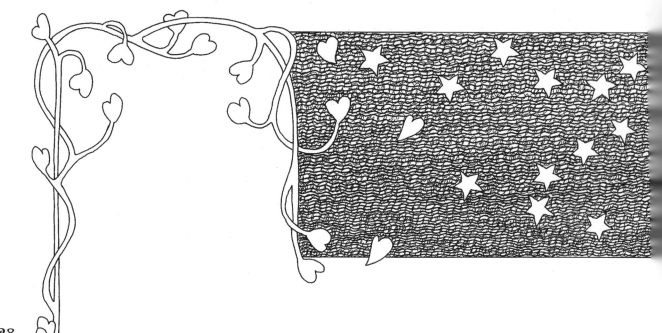

*Is it so small a thing
To have enjoyed the sun,
To have lived light in
  the spring,
To have loved,
To have thought,
To have done?*

Matthew Arnold

But for a tiny white tube emerging from his right nostril and taped to his cheek, one would not guess this baby is dying. His face is round and his cheeks are full. If his body is thin, it is hidden under his blue snap-up sleeper. His mother has changed his diaper but it was not wet. The baby has had no fluids for three days.

Brennan is quiet, his breath is soft. His father tells me the

child no longer cries. When the time came that Brennan was no longer able to suckle, the tube was inserted through his nose and advanced into his stomach. Sustenance could then be injected through the tubing with a syringe. But alas, three days before, even small amounts of formula trickled into the baby's stomach, bubbled up again into his mouth. The anxious parents summoned help. "What can we do?" the mother asked the doctor. And he answered with a sigh, "Nothing."

*Outside the open window
The morning air is all awash
  with angels.*

— Richard Wilbur

*Our birth is but a sleep and a
  forgetting;
The Soul that rises with us,
  our life's Star,
Hath had elsewhere its setting,
And cometh from afar;
Not in entire forgetfulness,
And not in utter nakedness,
But trailing clouds of glory do
  we come,
From God who is our home.*

— William Wordsworth

Passively, the baby looks out the window. It is as if vision flows from his eyes and he beholds images hidden from the grownups in the

room. He sees heaven. The angel-Brennan hovers near the baby-Brennan, indeed the angel streams into the child as radiant light, the two blending to become one. The baby begins his separation from the earth plane, the angel reclaims its own.

The baby always knew he would not stay long in this small body, his ego is yet unformed and fragile as a delicate membrane, allowing him the ability to perceive both sides, heaven and earth. As humans mature, their egos take root and grow dense. In time, humans learn to relate to the world exclusively through their bodies and egos until they forget their vast existences before and beyond their brief incarnations. They come to think they are their bodies. And they are not sure what will become of them when their bodies die and decay. Sometimes

Yet the timeless in you is aware of life's timelessness,
  And knows that yesterday is but today's memory and tomorrow is today's dream.
  And that which sings and contemplates in you is still dwelling within the bounds of that first moment which scattered the stars into space.

Kahlil Gibran

their angels communicate to them in hunches, ideas that come upon awakening from slumber, in intuition. And sometimes the humans listen.

The baby gazes out the window and watches as a legion of angels gathers to welcome him. The life of the mortal child flickers like a guttering candle.

Brennan, sweet boy, your travels here are nigh through. Say your farewell and come

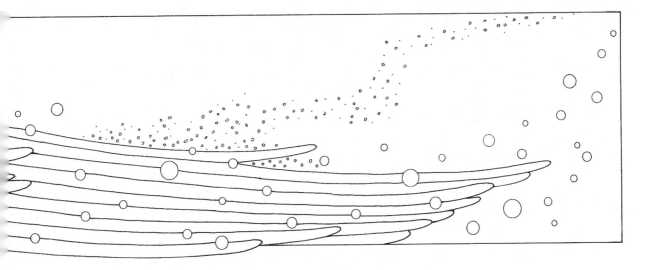

home to me for I am your soul and we are a splendid angel awaiting adventures on our journey back to the heart of God.

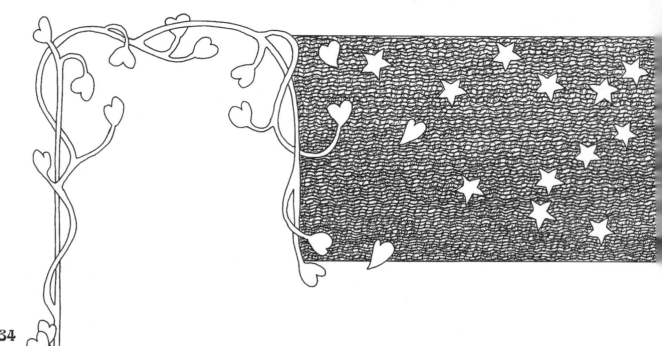

When you are sorrowful look again in your heart, and you shall see that in truth you are weeping for that which has been your delight.

Kahlil Gibran

The doctors cannot identify the malady that is stealing Brennan away. Physicians love to pinpoint things, to name them, to put them into categories. They cannot always cure or diminish the disorders they name but they can sometimes say, this is what

occurred and these are the chances it will repeat itself. Brennan does not fit into a category, something is wrong but it has no label. "We don't know," the father says, "if it could happen again. My wife is ready to have another baby," he pauses, "… but she isn't ready to lose another one." Nor is he.

What were their dreams for this child? Would he have been fair and vibrant like his mother? Would he have been dark and handsome, would he have grown up to be a fireman like his father? Did they wonder if he would play the piano, would he have loved baseball? "We had a name picked out early on," his father says, "but as the time of his birth grew near we changed it… I don't know why, but we felt we needed a gentler name. So we called him Brennan." It seems prophetic, I think to myself.

When love beckons to you, follow him,
  Though his ways are hard and steep.
  And when his wings enfold you yield to him,
  Though the sword hidden among his pinions may wound you.
  And when he speaks to you believe in him,
  Though his voice may shatter your dreams as the north wind lays waste the garden.

Kahlil Gibran

The angel Brennan loves this man well, this man who has done all he could do, given all he could give for his family, for his young son. But there is nothing to be done, the story is written.

The mother returns to the hospital. She carries her infant to the makeshift bed in the room that has become their temporary home. She curls herself around her child, flesh of her own, her body propped with her arm as a support, her elbow dug into the mattress. This woman has known her baby longer than anyone has, for she knew him even before her menses were interrupted, as her waistline thickened with pregnancy and her breasts grew tender and her stomach voiced a timid complaint. She had felt him quicken, and followed the progress of a growing fetus… the first flutterings in the second trimester, then the assertive heel and elbow sliding like a ripple under the surface of her skin, seeking comfort in the tight quarters of her belly. And she would caress him through the tissue and muscle of her abdomen and she would imagine holding him, remem-

For even as love crowns you so shall he crucify you.

Even as he is for your growth so is he for your pruning.

Even as he ascends to your height and caresses your tenderest branches that quiver in the sun,

So shall he descend to your roots and shake them in their clinging to the earth.

Kahlil Gibran

bering how small newborns are, how vulnerable with their quavering mewling cries. "Oh, feel him," she would say to the father as the elbow slid past her stretched navel, and they would laugh at the vigor of their tiny child.

Brennan the Eternal watches as the parents remember. He feels their sadness, he knows their love.

Beautiful woman, let me rock you as you once rocked me, let me sing you a lullaby to soften the hurt. Oh cry for the human mother whose heart aches for her baby, but through the tears remember why we came to this place and let it deepen you.

Beloved father, let me touch the brow that knits when you remember the baby who will die this night in your arms; weep to ease the father's loss, but do not cry for the angel who crept into your life and opened your heart. Didn't we do well?

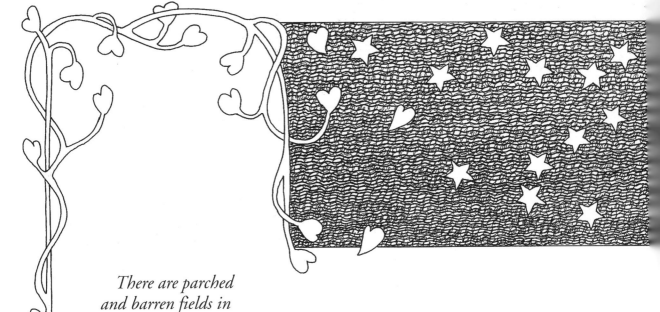

*There are parched
and barren fields in
our lives.
   There is autumn in
our existence.
   But these are the
grounds of our growth,
   the seed-beds of our
miracles.
   In these fields we
will someday blossom,
   and the innocence of
the world will return
with our own.*

Richard Caniell

At nine o'clock in the evening I am summoned to the room, Brennan's breathing has changed. It is the dying breath. It comes in short

gasping efforts with a heave of the chest, although the baby does not particularly appear to labor. He is warning them that time is short. "I do not know how long it will be," I tell them. "I am accustomed to adults and the elderly who can go on like this for hours, for a day or longer. I do not know about babies." And I can tell them no more.

The breathy heaving continues long. A young nurse works near me tonight; she is the age of Brennan's parents and is involved with the events in this room because she has a tender heart. We take turns listening at the door to Brennan's breathing, and for a long while it does not change. But now it is a little more urgent and intense. Hesitantly, I slip into the darkened room. The mother appears to be sleeping. I move quietly past the father's bed to the crib. It is empty! Startled,

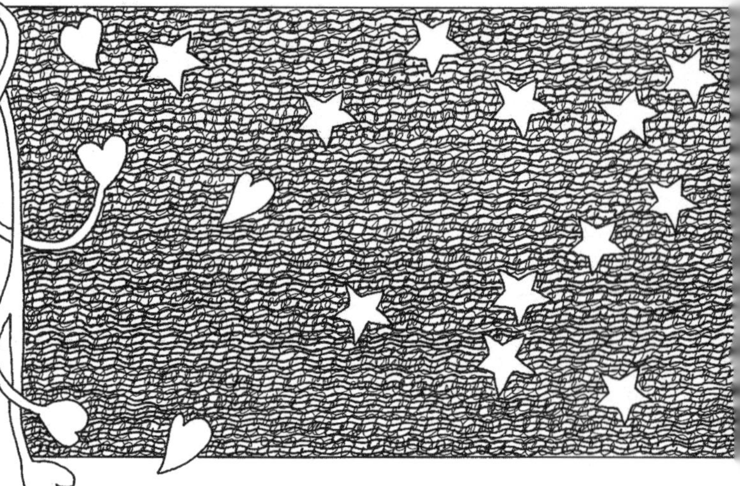

When the spirit is ready,
When everything is ready,
Fresh and simple—
As achieved and plain
As sunflowers
In a jar reddened by sun,
Then let it come.

Lucile Adler

I turn quickly to see the father passively observing me, the baby lying on his chest, supported by his arm crooked around the child. A brief communication and silent messages of regard pass between us. I leave them.

It is near the end of my shift. At ten o'clock, I ask the young nurse to keep watch while I leave briefly to give report to the night shift. I

have just returned when the mother again beckons me to the room. I know from her eyes what awaits me. The baby still lies in the hammock of his father's arm and the father's eyes mirror the mother's. Brennan's face is placid, his eyes are softly closed, the rosebud lips pink, the tiny tube coiled and secured to the silk of his cheek. But the gulping breaths are more abrupt and shallow, the intervals between them longer, and though he works harder, he does not draw sufficient air to sustain life in the small body. Together we watch the breathing pattern slow… and finally cease. And he is gone.

*The deeper the sorrow
the less tongue it hath.*

The Talmud

Steadfast, the mother lifts her baby from the father's chest. She lays him in the crib and pulls his small quilt over him, the quilt he will never

outgrow. The room is dark. Facing her husband, she sits at the foot of his bed with her legs outstretched, paralleling his legs. He rests with the head of the bed lifted to a semi-sitting position. They are silent with occasional murmurings connecting them. The tears are sparse now, already dried, they have been shed abundantly over the past half year, with a savage wrenching and rending of their hearts. Numbness has at last settled over them like a sedative, clouding reality.

The angel Brennan watches the father's nurse making telephone calls. She wants this matter settled before she goes home tonight. Her fierce mother-instinct is aroused and she will not relinquish this family to strangers. She is told no one will be sent from the funeral home tonight, they will come in the morning. Frustrated, she argues to no avail,

For what is it to die but to stand naked in the wind and to melt into the sun?
And what is it to cease breathing, but to free the breath from its restless tides, that it may rise and expand and seek God unencumbered?

Kahlil Gibran

asking that the child be taken to the mortuary directly from the room where he died. Wouldn't that be easier on the parents, she reasons? How can they rest tonight knowing their baby's body lies in a cold vault just down the hall from where they sleep?

The angel knows the nurse worries too much, it

is the human thing to do. She is unsure of how long to leave the child with the parents; they seem stunned and it is hard for her to read them. She does not want to rob them of precious time never to be retrieved. Nor does she want them waiting, wondering, wishing it done.

After a time, she gathers a flannel sheet and folds it into a square. She enters the room and moves to the crib. Wordlessly the younger nurse follows her. Lifting the baby onto the flannel sheet, she swaddles him as if in a receiving blanket, leaving his face exposed. He is tender and warm and she draws him to her body supporting his sweet head… now he is hers, this is her domain. The mother and father acknowledge the moment and bid their child adieu.

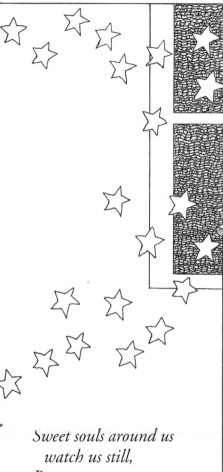

*Sweet souls around us
watch us still,
Press nearer to our
side;
Into our thoughts, into
our prayers,
With gentle helpings
glide.*

Harriet Beecher Stowe

Brennan, now merged and absorbed into the grand angel, feels only curiosity as he follows the two nurses on their mission. The young woman carries the key to the room that is their destination. Both women's eyes glisten with tears. "I've never seen a baby that wasn't alive," the younger nurse says, just now realizing this truth. "Nor have I," answers the father's nurse, and she holds the baby closer to

her woman's body, a body that has borne two children who are now grown and are a joy to her.

What if he is not really dead, she wonders, for his face is not waxen and slack. These two have witnessed the visage of death countless times, and death is clearly evident in the bodies of the aged. But it is elusive in the winsome face of this tender babe… she looks again for the movement of air coming and going. Brennan looks too, but only to see what she sees. He knows the body is vacant, the inhabitant breathes with Spirit now.

The nurse studies the baby's face as if to memorize it. Softly, she strokes his cheek with the back of her forefinger. Gently, she lifts a lid so she may know his eye color. She feels the

If you would indeed behold the spirit of death, open your heart wide unto the body of life.

For life and death are one, even as the river and the sea are one.

Kahlil Gibran

fine texture of his hair between her thumb and fingers. But it is getting late. Upon rearranging and adjusting the flannel sheeting to insure his warmth and comfort, the two nurses reluctantly leave the baby. In the room, they leave the light burning.

While grief is fresh, every attempt to divert it only irritates.

Samuel Johnson

Should you shield the canyons from the windstorms you would never see the true beauty of their carvings.

Elisabeth Kübler-Ross

Midnight approaches and Good Friday is nearly over. Funny, we do not know when we wake in the morning what turns our lives may take in the course of the day. I am drained. I have spent my

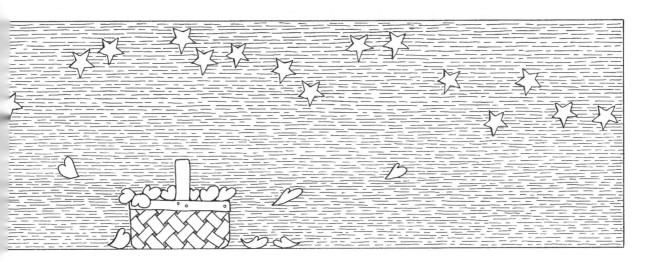

emotional energy. I feel no sadness, no anguish, no relief, no peace. I am empty. The house is dark but for the moon and porch lights filtering through the windows. Just as it seemed necessary to leave the lamp burning for Brennan, I now find the dark is soothing to me. I sit on a knee-high stool in my kitchen, leaning against a cabinet, my jacket still buttoned, my bag still draped over my shoulder. I look out into the yard, but I see only emptiness. I do not know what to do with the emptiness. Yet I do not want to fill myself with the trivial noise of the world. I do not know how long I sit there.

Brennan is dead. My heart is stagnant, clotted with feelings I do not understand.

The weekend passes. On Saturday, the mother moves home to spend more time with her other child whose baby brother

In every winter's heart there is a quivering spring, and behind the veil of each night there is a smiling dawn.

Kahlil Gibran

will never come home. The rollaway bed is folded up like a peanut butter sandwich and stashed against the wall, a reminder that the family is together though divided just now. Brennan's quilt drapes over its side. The crib is gone, returned to the pediatric storeroom.

The mother and son visit each day and the father's recovery progresses. Easter comes and goes, its message is not unnoticed. On Monday, when I ar-

rive at work, I find a basket of plants in bloom left there by the parents, and cards for the nurses. But the family has gone home. In a few day's time I too will leave for vacation to be away from here and to reflect on the events of this weekend.

Summer has come. The tantalizing burst of spring blends into the full-bodied green of summer. Brennan has been with me each day since our meeting, I do not know why. I look for him in the faces of every baby I see. Sometimes I think I see the round face or the fair hair… none have the enchanting rosebud mouth. Sometimes I tell his story to another, and my tears flow. And I laugh and say, "I do not know where the tears come from," and the listener smiles through moist eyes. Perhaps it is a cellular thing, the mother with empty arms, the dad, power-

*I have come back
again to where I
belong;
not an enchanted
place, but the walls
are strong.*

Dorothy H. Rath

*If I keep a green
bough in my heart,
the singing bird will
come.*

Chinese Proverb

less to protect his young. Some days Brennan slips in to remind me that love is real and there is hope for human beings. Sometimes he springs in for a quick hello, a cookies-and-milk visit. Lately when I write of him, I search my mind for just the right word, and it comes to me on angel's wings.

I had brought the basket with its colorful flowers home with me, feeling a bit like the

greedy child who nabs the candy before other fingers have the chance. But I wanted to have a part of this family in my home.

The plants brightened my counter top for a time until they grew cramped in the small basket, their blossoms dying back, then I repotted them in a planter on my porch outside the sliding glass door.

The geraniums are getting their second wind and will burst forth any day. The ivy is trying to go unnoticed until it can spill over the side and surprise me, but I am on to it. The slugs made breakfast of the marigolds. I should have protected them by putting them in a hanging basket, but I wanted to keep this troop of plants together. Silly woman. Well, I guess they had their day. I added some yellow violas to stand in for them.

But the pansies bring pride to flowerdom. They are hearty

When the Light of Life falls upon the life of men, secret powers begin to unfold, sleeping perceptions begin to awake, and the whole being becomes alive unto God.

John Henry Jowett

For he will give his angels charge of you to guard you in all your ways.

Psalms 91:11

and prolific, having sprung forth an impressive brood whose purple and white faces wave happily with the mildest currents of air.

The parents write to me. The mother pens her rounded script, "When I am feeling sad I go into Brennan's room and before long I always feel warmer inside."

Brennan's father has been granted an extraordinary gift by this baby, his son. "I have

seen how Brennan touched those around us," he writes, "and our lives are fuller for having known him but for a short time. Through him, I have seen the spirit of goodness in our fellow people and I want to take the love I have received from Brennan and spread it to others." Like honey on dry bread, love sweetens, love enriches, it gives meaning to life and turns existence into living.

"We miss Brennan a lot," his mother writes, "but we know he is in a better place, playing ball and learning to fly. We both feel such peace now. I guess we all have an angel watching out for us and it feels so good." Yes. Oh yes, it does.

Brennan is free, loosed from the bondage of faulty flesh. He moves with the angels now and my heart is consoled.

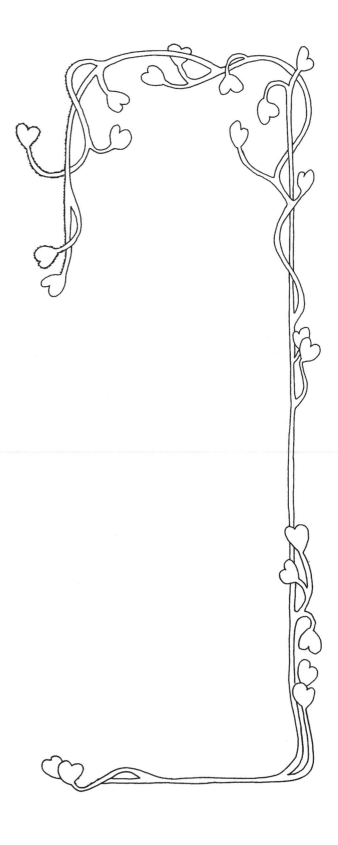

Appendix

62

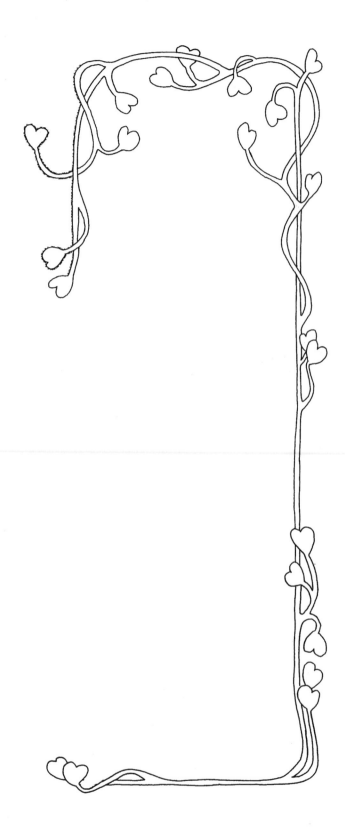

RESOURCE LIST

Support Groups:

The Compassionate Friends, Inc.
P.O. Box 3696, Oak Brook, IL 60522-3696
Phone: 630-990-0010
E-mail: tcf_national@prodigy.com
http://www.compassionatefriends.org

Pen-Parents, Inc.
P.O. Box 8738, Reno, NV 89507-8738
Phone: 702-826-7332
E-mail: penparents@penparents.org
http://www.penparents.org

Bereavement and Hospice Support Netline
University of Baltimore, Yale Gordon College of Liberal Arts
1420 N. Charles Street, Baltimore, Maryland 21201-5779
http://www.ubalt.edu/www/bereavement

SHARE: The National SHARE Office
St. Joseph Health Center, 300 First Capitol Drive
St. Charles, Missouri 63301-2893
Phone: 314-947-6164 • 1-800-821-6819
E-mail: share@nationalshareoffice.com
www.nationalShareOffice.com

SIDS Network
PO Box 520, Ledyard, Connecticut 06339
Phone: 860-892-7042 X551
E-mail: sidsnet@sids-network.org
http://www.sids-network.org
SIDS electronic newsletter, Reaching Out

Alive Alone: An organization for parents left completely childless
Kay Bevington, Alive Alone
11115 Dull Robinson Road, Van Wert, OH. 45891
E-mail: alivalon@bright.net
http://www.bright.net/~alivalon
Newsletter

Bereaved Parents of the USA
PO Box 95, Park Forest, Illinois 60466
Phone: 217-241-HOPE • 708-748-7672
E-mail: hope@fgi.net
http://www.bereavedparentsusa.org

Dougy Center
P. O. Box 86852, Portland, Oregon 97286
Phone: 503-775-5683
E-mail: help@dougy.org
www.dougy.org

Associations and Newsletters

Association of Birth Defect Children
930 Woodcock Rd, Suite 225, Orlando, FL 32803
Phone: 407-245-7035
24 hr hotline: 1-800-313-2232
Email: abdc@birthdefects.org
http://www.birthdefects.org

National Sudden Infant Death Syndrome Resource Center
2070 Chain Bridge Road, Suite 450, Vienna, VA 22182
Phone: 703-821-8955
E-mail: sids@circsol.com
http://www.circsol.com/sids

Children's Hospice International
2202 Mt. Vernon Avenue, Suite 3C, Alexandria, VA 22301
Phone: 1-800-24CHILD
E-mail chiorg@aol.com
http://www.chionline.org
Quarterly newsletter

Hospice Foundation of America
2001 S. St., Suite 300, Washington DC 20009
Phone: 202-638-5419
E-mail: hfa@hospicefoundation.org
http://www.hospicefoundation.org
Newsletter: Journeys

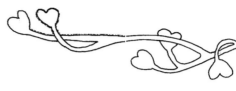

Pediatric AIDS Foundation
2950 31st Street, Ste. 125, Santa Monica, CA 90405
Phone: 310-314-1459 • 1-888-499-4673
E-mail: info@pedaids.org
http://www.pedaids.org

Recommended Reading

John Bramblett, *When Good-bye is Forever: Learning to Live Again After the Loss of a Child.* A father's personal story. New York: Ballantine Books, 1991.

Elisabeth Kubler-Ross, *Remember the Secret.* Milbrae, CA: Celestial Arts, reprint ed. 1998. Illustrated children's book.

Leo Buscaglia, PhD., *The Fall of Freddie the Leaf: A Story of Life for All Ages.* New York: C. B. Slack, Inc., 1982. (Illustrated children's book).

Molly Fumia, *Safe Passage, Words to Help the Grieving Hold Fast and Let Go.* Emeryville, CA: Conari Press, 1992.

Martha Whitmore Hickman, *Healing After Loss, Daily Meditations for Working through Grief.* New York: Avon Books, 1994.

James Jennings, *Big George: The Autobiography of an Angel.* Carson CA: Hay House, 1995. Fiction.

Carol Staudacher, *A Time to Grieve, Meditations for Healing After the Death of a Loved One*, San Francisco: Harper San Francisco, 1994.

Elizabeth Mehren, *After the Darkest Hour, the Sun Will Shine Again, A parents guide to coping with the loss of a child.* New York: Simon & Schuster, 1997.

Rana K. Limbo and Sara Rich Wheeler, *When a Baby Dies: A Handbook for Healing and Helping.* La Crosse, WI: RTS Bereavement Services, 1986.

Johann Christoph Arnold. *I Tell You a Mystery: Life, Death, and Eternity.* Farmington, PA: The Plough Publishing House, 1996.

Joan Hagan Arnold and Penelope Buschman Gemma, *A Child Dies: A Portrait of Family Grief,* Second Edition. Philadelphia, PA: The Charles Press, 1994.

Barbara D. Rosof, *The Worst Loss: How Families Heal from the Death of a Child.* New York: Henry Holt and Company, Inc., 1994.

Katherine Fair Donnelly, *Recovering from the Loss of a Child.* New York: Macmillan, 1982.

Harriet Sarnoff Schiff, *The Bereaved Parent.* New York: Crown Publishers, 1977. Reprint edition, Viking Press, 1998.

Judith R. Bernstein, *When the Bough Breaks: Forever After the Death of a Son or Daughter.* Kansas City, MO: Andrews & McMeel, 1997.

Ann K. Finkbeiner, *After the Death of a Child: Living With Loss Through the Years.* New York: Free Press, 1996.

Quote References

Most of the quotes in this book are taken from the original works of the authers, which are often out of print. However, if you would like to read more from a certain writer, the following books are recommended.

Page 8: Henri Frédéric Amiel (1821-1881)
Weaver, Janet L and Dixon, Virginia. *Tender Thoughts*. Bloomington, MN: Garborg's Heart 'n Home, Inc., 1996.

Page 10: Ralph Waldo Emerson (1803-1882)
Weaver, Janet L and Dixon, Virginia. *Tender Thoughts*. Bloomington, MN: Garborg's Heart 'n Home, Inc., 1996.

Page 12: Hannah More
From Fitzhenry, Robert I., (Ed.) *The Harper Book of Quotations*. New York: HarperPerennial, 1993, page 160.

Page 14: Horatius Bonar (1808-1889)
Bachelder, Louise, (Ed.) *On Serenity*. Mount Vernon, NY: The Peter Pauper Press, Inc., 1974.

Page 16: Langston Hughes (1902-1967)
From Hughes, Langston. *Collected Poems*. Copyright © 1994 by Estate of Langston Houges. Reprinted by permission of Alfred A. Knopf Inc.

Page 18: Sigurd F. Olson (1899-1982)
From Olson, Sigurd F. *Reflections From the North Country*. New York: Alfred A. Knopf, 1990, page 117.

Page 18: Elizabeth Barrett Browning (1806-1861)
Whitley, Ben W. and Weaver, John C. *Quiet Thoughts: Reflections on the Meaning of Life.* Kansas City, MO: Hallmark Crown Edition, 1971.

Page 20: Roderick MacLeish
From *Prince Ombra.* New York: Tom Doherty Associates, Inc., St. Martin's Press, 1994, page 14.

Page 22: A Course in Miracles
From *A Course in Miracles., Vol. I.* Farmingdale, NT: Foundation for Inner Peace, 1975, page 446. *A Course in Miracles*® copyright © 1975, 1992, reprint by permission of Foundation for *A Course in Miracles.*

Page 24: Susan Mark Spalding
From a greeting card by *Flavia Romantics.* Santa Barbara, CA: Flavia Publishing, Inc.

Page 26: Blaise Pascal (1623-1662)
Whitley, Ben W. and Weaver, John C. *Quiet Thoughts: Reflections on the Meaning of Life.* Kansas City, MO: Hallmark Crown Edition, 1971.

Page 28: Matthew Arnold (1822-1888)
Whitley, Ben W. and Weaver, John C. *Quiet Thoughts: Reflections on the Meaning of Life.* Kansas City, MO: Hallmark Crown Edition, 1971.

Page 30: Richard Wilbur
From *Things of This World: Poems by Richard Wilbur.* New York: Harcourt, Brace & Co., 1956, page 5.

Page 30: William Wordsworth (1770-1850)
Jeffares, A. Norman and Gray, Martin. *Dictionary of Quotations,* Glasgow: Harper Collins, 1995.

Page 32, 34, 36, 38, 46, 50, 54: Kahlil Gibran (1883-1931)
From *The Prophet* by Kahlil Gibran. Copyright © 1923 by Kahlil Gibran and renewed 1951 by Administrators CTA of Kahlil Gibran Estate and Mary G. Gibran. Reprinted by permission of Alfred A. Knopf, Inc.

Page 40: Richard Caniell
From Jones, Dewitt. *What the Road Passes by* by Richard Craniel. Copyright © 1978, Graphic Arts Center Publication, Portland, Oregon.

Page 42: Lucile Adler
From *The Ripening Light: Selected Poems 1977-1987*, Layton, UT: Gibbs-Smith Publisher. A Peregrine Smith Book. From the poem *The Last Day*, page 80-81.

Page 44: The Talmud
From Fitzhenry, Robert I., (Ed.) *The Harper Book of Quotations*. New York: HarperPerennial, 1993.

Page 48: Harriet Beecher Stowe (1811-1896)
Gail Harvey (comp.), *On the Wings of Angels*. New York: Avenel/Gramercy Books, 1993.

Page 52: Samuel Johnson (1709-1784)
From Fitzhenry, Robert I., (Ed.) *The Harper Book of Quotations*. New York: HarperPerennial, 1993.

Page 52: Elisabeth Kübler-Ross
From Fitzhenry, Robert I., (Ed.) *The Harper Book of Quotations*. New York: HarperPerennial, 1993.

Page 56: Dorothy H. Rath
From Fitzhenry, Robert I., (Ed.) *The Harper Book of Quotations*. New York: HarperPerennial, 1993.

Page 56: Chinese Proverb
Whitley, Benjamin. *Quiet Thoughts*: *Reflections on the Meaning of Life*. Kansas City, MO: Hallmark Crown Edition, 1971.

Page 58: John Henry Jowett (1864-1923)
The Episteles of Peter. Grand Rapids: Kregel Publications, 1993.

Page 58: Psalms
The Holy Bible. New York: Oxford University Press, 1898.